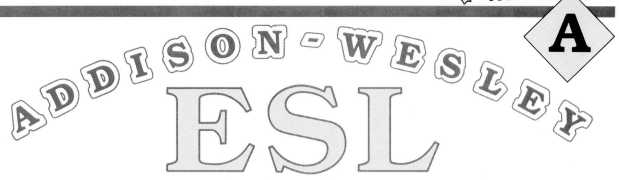

ADDISON-WESLEY
ESL

A

Michael Walker

Original Music by Bob Schneider

Addison-Wesley Publishing Company

Reading, Massachusetts • Menlo Park, California • New York • Don Mills, Ontario • Wokingham, England
Amsterdam • Bonn • Sydney • Singapore • Tokyo • Madrid • San Juan

Contents

A Publication of the World Language Division

Editor-in-Chief: Judith Bittinger

Project Director: Elinor Chamas

Editorial Development: Elly Schottman, Talbot Hamlin

Production/Manufacturing: James W. Gibbons

Design, Art Direction, and Production: Taurins Design Associates, New York

Cover Art: John Sandford

Illustrators: Teresa Anderko 12, 16, 32, 50, 54, 60; Yvette Banek 22, 23, 66, 70, 71; Ray Cruz 10; Diane Teske Harris 42, 76, 77, 78, 79; Meryl Henderson 63; Design Five 28, 34, 46, 47, 74; Susan Lexa 9, 43, 51, 68; Ben Mahan 8; Sharron O'Neil 40; Diane Paterson 6, 30, 33, 67, 73; John Sandford 26, 44, 56, 57, 58, 59, 60; Karen Schmidt 36, 37, 38, 39; Jerry Smath 3, 5, 7, 11, 13, 14, 21, 25, 29, 41, 45, 49, 55, 61, 62, 65, 69, 80; Sally Springer 4, 15, 24, 53; John Wallner 18, 19; Marsha Winborn 20, 27, 31, 52, 64, 72

Photographers: Ken Lax 35, 48, 55, 75; Peter Tenzer 17.

ISBN 0-201-57810-7

3 4 5 6 7 8 9 10 11 12-DA-96 95 94 93 92

Time for School

boy   girl   teacher   chair   table

Greeting/identifying people
Describing location

3

♪♪ TPR chant
Following directions
Counting

TPR
Following directions
Sequencing

Around School

one   two   three   four   five

Asking/giving directions
Identifying school locations

At Home

sofa   TV   phone   bed   bathtub

The Salt and Pepper Shake

and

and

Put your

On your

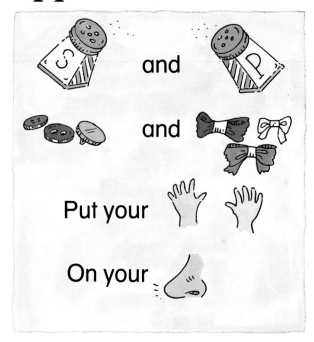

and

and

Put your

On your

Describing people/things/actions

Listening Comprehension

Word Game

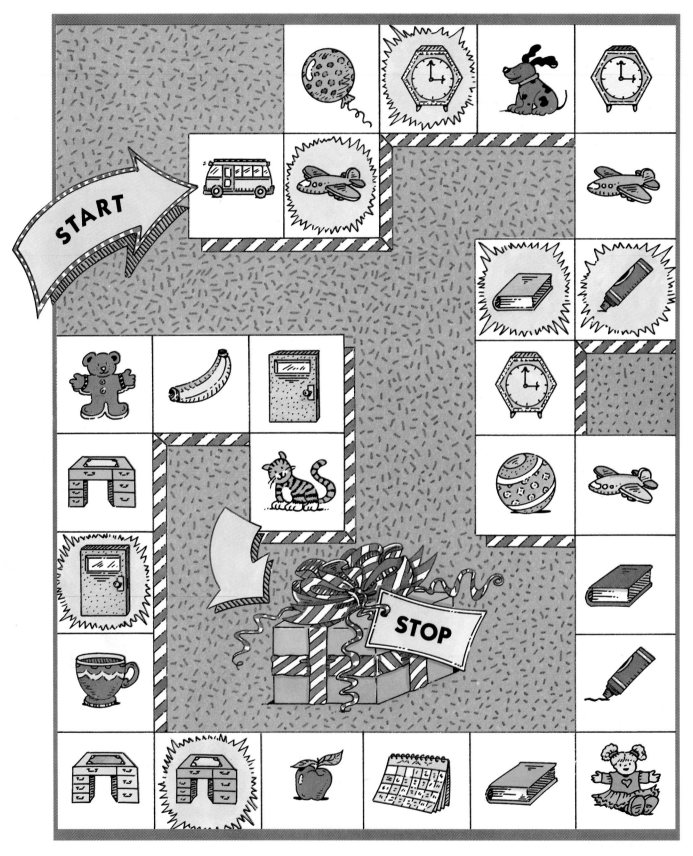

Vocabulary Progress Check, Units 1–3
Socializing/turn-taking

Content Skills

The Farmer and the Beet

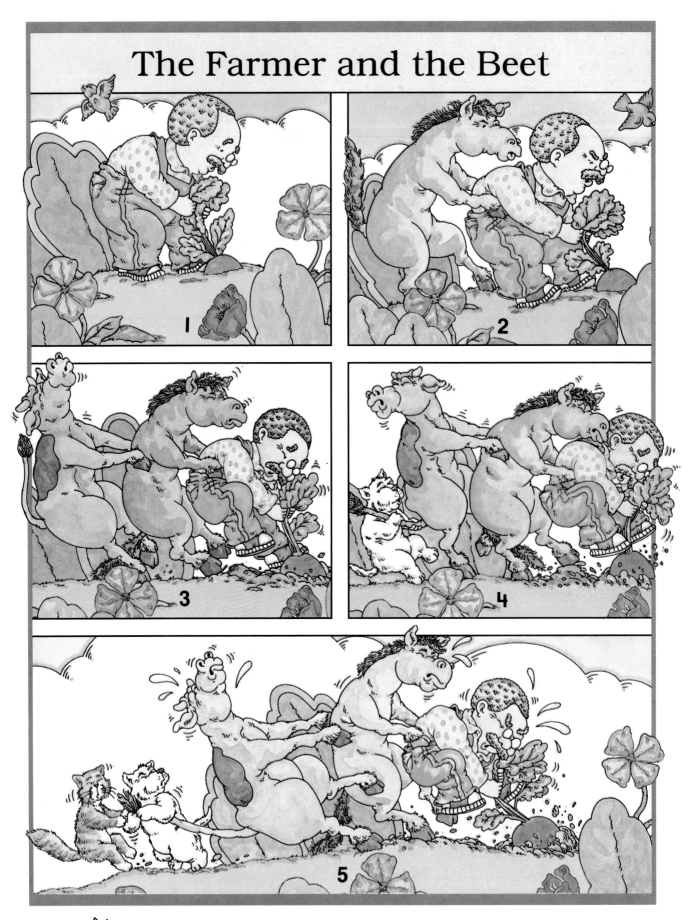

Literature: Traditional tale
Shared reading; role play

If You're Happy and You Know It

TPR song
Expressing feelings

Having Fun

dress **skirt** **jacket** **sweater** **shirt**

Describing clothing
Asking/giving information

Describing actions

What Do You See?

turtle   fish   frog   duck   bird

Identifying animals/location/quantity   25

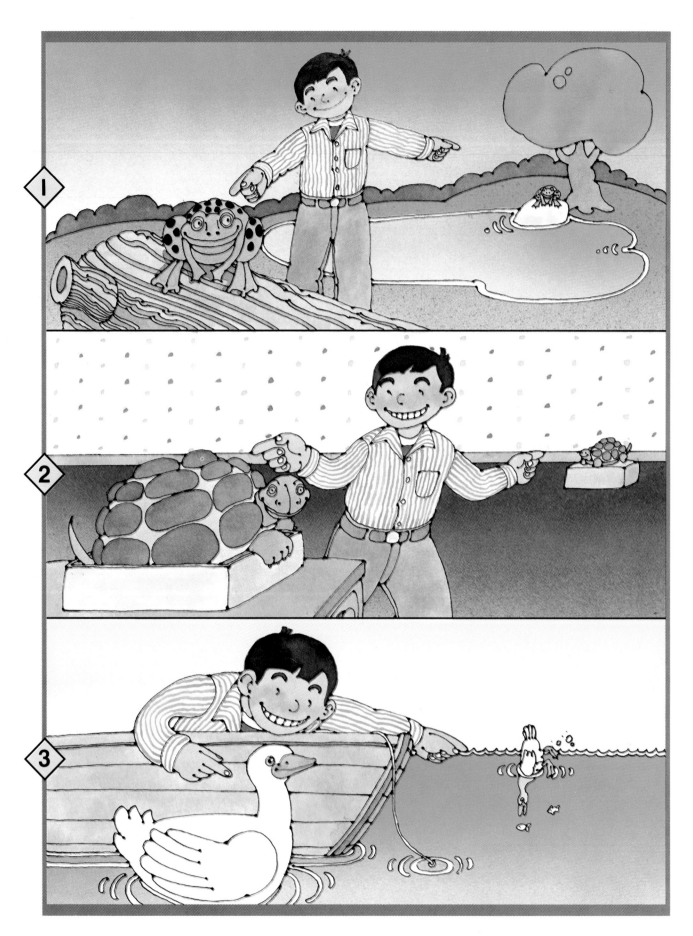

Identifying location

1   a   b   c

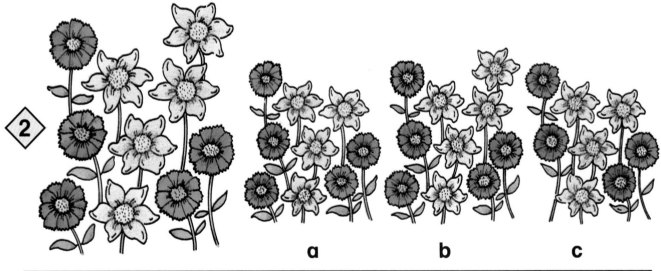

2   a   b   c

3   a   b   c

Identifying same/different
Describing people / objects

People and Places

| doctor | mail carrier | firefighter | police officer | bus driver |

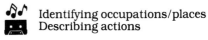 Identifying occupations/places
Describing actions

Today, Today, Today

Action song; role play
Creating new verses

1	DAN'S RESTAURANT	Sunday	
2	SHOES BAKERY TOYS	Monday	
3	POST OFFICE	Tuesday	
4	LIBRARY	Wednesday	
5		Thursday	
6	SUPERMARKET SPECIAL! 89¢ SALE!	Friday	
7	ZOO	Saturday	

Identifying days of the week
Describing actions

Listening Comprehension

1

a   b   c

2

a   b   c

3

a   b   c

4

a   b   c

5

a   b   c

Word Game

Vocabulary Progress Check, Units 4–6
Socializing/turn-taking
Describing location

What is the color of your hair ?

Red   Donny   Bill

Black   Jesse   Anna   Louis

Brown   Lisa   Linda   Maria

Blonde   Lilly   Jake   Susan

Goldilocks and the Three Bears

Once upon a time,
there were three bears.

Literature: Traditional tale
Shared reading; role play

The End

Three Little Monkeys

Traditional rhyme; role play

Food Fun

pour mix eat drink wash

Menu

$2.00

$3.00

$2.00

$2.00

$1.00

$1.00

$1.00

40¢

50¢

50¢

50¢

40¢

Asking/giving information
Expressing likes/dislikes
Polite requests

taco
shells

beef

cheese

lettuce

tomatoes

Peanut Butter and Jelly Song

Sequencing
Describing quantity

Around Town

bank   drugstore   laundromat   toy store   gas station

Asking/giving information
Identifying means of transportation

Asking/giving information
Identifying animals

Busy Days

eight
o'clock

nine
o'clock

ten
o'clock

eleven
o'clock

twelve
o'clock

Sequencing   Describing school routines   49

Do You? Do You? Do You?

Daily routines song; role play

Describing/comparing

Listening Comprehension

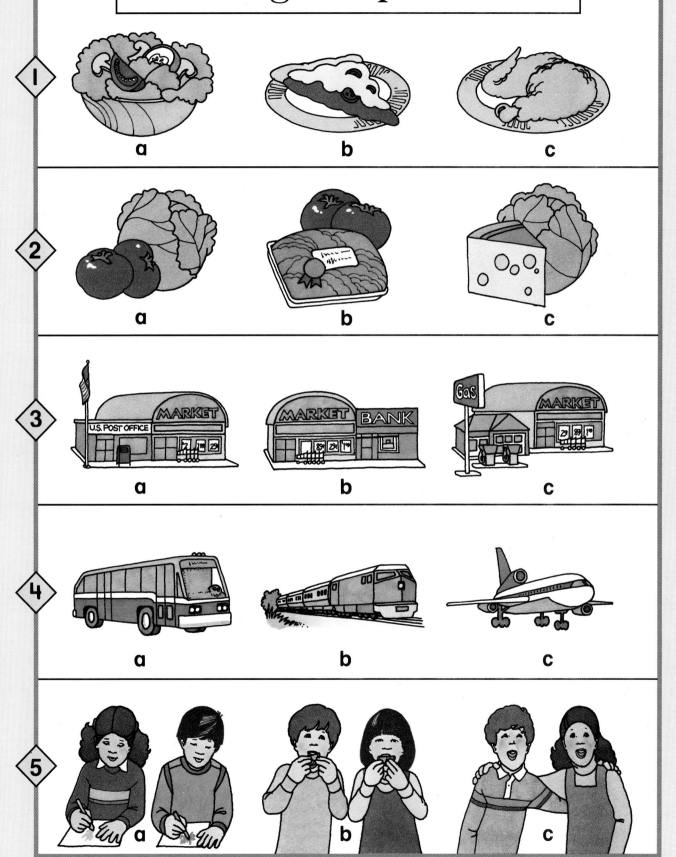

Word Game

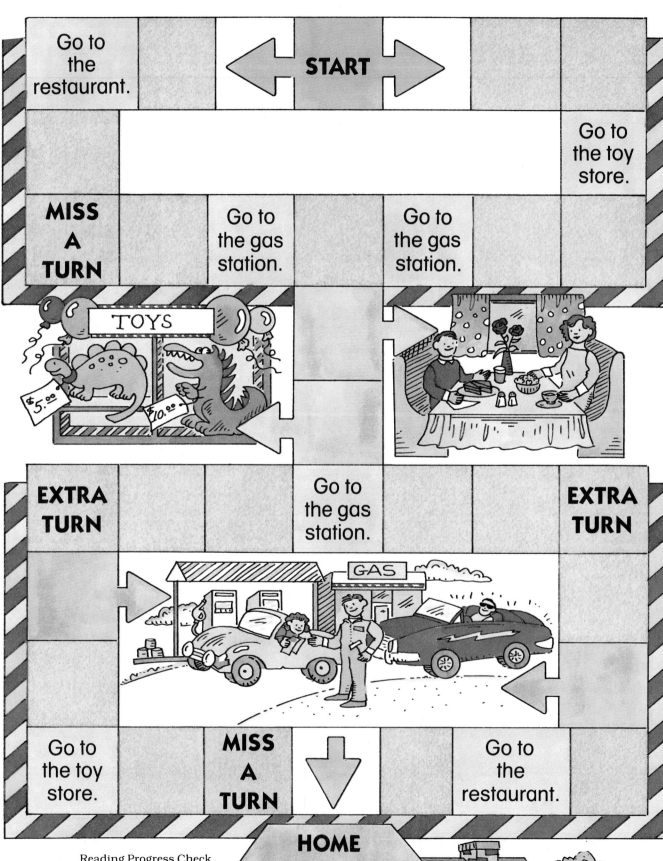

Go to the restaurant.

START

Go to the toy store.

MISS A TURN

Go to the gas station.

Go to the gas station.

TOYS

$5.00

$10.00

EXTRA TURN

Go to the gas station.

EXTRA TURN

GAS

Go to the toy store.

MISS A TURN

Go to the restaurant.

HOME

Reading Progress Check,
Units 7–9
Socializing/turn-taking

Which one is taller?

Which one is heavier?   Which one is faster?

The Gingerbread Man

Once upon a time, a woman made a .

"Run, run, run!"

Literature: Traditional tale
Shared reading; role play

"Run, run, run!"

"Run, run, run!"

"Stop! Stop! Stop!"

That was the end of the  !

The Wheels on the Bus

60   Action song; role play

On the Farm

horse   cow   chicken   pig   barn

Describing actions/ability
Cause and effect

Friday is day.

Mike and his mom make every Friday.

1. He washes the .

2. She cuts the .

3. She puts the in a .

4. She stirs with a .

5. It smells good!

6. It tastes good, too.

Asking/giving information
Recalling details

How's the Weather?

umbrella   steps   traffic light   puddle   crosswalk

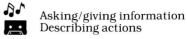

Asking/giving information
Describing actions

Sequencing
Describing actions

It's spring.

It's summer.

It's fall.

It's winter.

Asking/giving information
Identifying seasons/seasonal activities

Now and Then

baby   puppy   tadpole   kitten   caterpillar

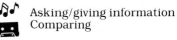

Asking/giving information
Comparing

69

This is Tony.

This is what Tony did after school.

---

1. He took the bus home.

2. He hugged his cat.

---

3. He played with his baby sister.

4. He ate dinner.

---

5. He brushed his teeth.

6. He went to sleep with his bear.

Describing actions
Retelling a story

This is Kim.

This is what Kim did after school.

1. She walked home.

2. She helped her grandmother.

3. She painted a picture.

4. She ate dinner.

5. She took a bath.

6. She went to sleep with her bunny.

She can do it now.

1

He can do it now.

2

They can do it now.

3

Listening Comprehension

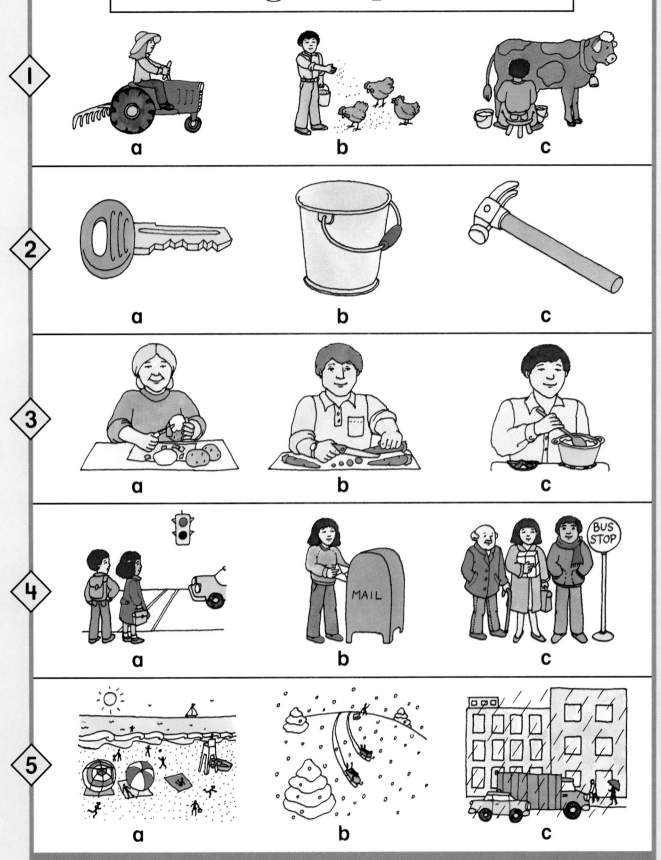

Word Game

horse

shoe

soup

pig

jacket

cow

apple

celery

shirt

sweater

lemon

boots

dog

chickens

milk

mittens

START

THE END

Reading Progress Check, Units 10–12
Socializing/turn-taking

The Three Little Pigs

Once upon a time,
there were three little pigs.

Little pig, little pig,
let me in, let me in.

Not by the hair on my chinney-chin-chin.

Then I'll **huff** and I'll **puff,**
And I'll **blow** your house in.

Literature: Traditional tale
Shared reading; role play

 Little pig, little pig,
let me in, let me in.

 Not by the hair on my chinney-chin-chin.

 Then I'll **huff** and I'll **puff,**
And I'll **blow** your house in.

 Little pig, little pig,
let me in, let me in.

 Not by the hair on my chinney-chin-chin.

 Then I'll **huff** and I'll **puff,**
And I'll **blow** your house in.

The End

Down on Grandpa's Farm

Traditional song; role play